OUT OF THE DEPTHS

Encountering Depression

GONVILLE FFRENCH-BEYTAGH

With an Epilogue by
WENDY ROBINSON

SLG Press
Convent of the Incarnation Fairacres
Parker Street Oxford OX4 1TB England

www.slgpress.co.uk

First published 1990

© THE SISTERS OF THE LOVE OF GOD 1990 & 2010
Second Edition 2010

Cover Illustration:
© *Original art work*: Sister Catherine SLG

SLG Press asserts:

(a) on behalf of Gonville ffrench-Beytagh, the moral right of Gonville ffrench-Beytagh to be identified as the author of the work, in accordance with Sections 77 & 78 of the Copyright, Designs and Patents Act 1988;

(b) on behalf of Wendy Robinson, the moral right of Wendy Robinson to be identified as the author of the Epilogue, in accordance with Sections 77 & 78 of the Copyright, Designs and Patents Act 1988;

(c) on behalf of Sister Catherine SLG, the moral right of Sister Catherine SLG to be identified as the original author of the artistic work on the cover, in accordance with Sections 77 & 78 of the Copyright, Designs and Patents Act 1988.

ISBN 978-0-7283-0183-2
ISSN 0307-1405

Printed by
Will Print, Oxford, England

TEN YEARS after my pamphlet *Facing Depression* was published, I had a bout of depression deeper and more severe than any I had ever experienced in my whole life, and when I tried to re-read the pamphlet I found that it really was not much use to me. There is nothing in it that is not true or valid; it just did not reach down into the depths of dread and darkness and despair into which I had descended. So I thought that it might be worthwhile trying to describe these depths.

The kind of depression I was now experiencing is not really describable. The difficulty is that when you are in the depths of depression you are quite unable to write—or indeed to do—anything about it; when you do slowly emerge from it, you cannot really remember how dreadful, how literally full of dread, it was. The great thing is that you do emerge, although at the time you believe you know with certainty that this time there is no hope or prospect of ever doing so. In fact, you don't even want to come through. All you want is oblivion. You want to be dead and have it all over and done with. You don't particularly want to die, but just to be dead. There seems to be no question of any life after death or anything like that. You are just not interested, and total oblivion is all that you want; and to be dead is the only possible way to complete oblivion.

The occasion and the cause of my massive depression were twofold, although there is a lot more to it than that. First, I had a slight stroke which affected my right-hand side and which slowed me down considerably, so I decided that it was time to retire. I had been a reasonably active parish priest for over forty years, both in Africa and in England, and at the age of seventy-four, retirement seemed to be the logical next step. Although I was aware that there is a very considerable

1

trauma involved in retiring from an active life, I had not realised the extent and depth of the trauma. The whole business of what is now called 'loss of role', and with that to some extent a loss of meaning and purpose, only gradually sink in. However kind people are, you begin to realize, or at least to suspect, that they *are* just being kind and no more. The perception grows upon you that you no longer really matter much.

The second cause or occasion of this depression was that I had to spend some months in hospital. I had three fairly major surgical operations, together with a rather nasty thing called ulcerative colitis and, finally, kidney failure. All this meant a certain amount of pain and quite long periods of hardly being aware of what was going on. Then it was supposed that I was dying and I was anointed (given the Sacrament of Unction). Eventually there began the long, slow process of recovery, where it was difficult to discern any progress from day to day. It is only when I look back over the months from the time when I was helpless in hospital to the present moment—home again and able to walk a bit and do some things for myself, however small—that I realize how much better I am. Then I began to appreciate how much I owed to doctors and nurses and friends who, under God, enabled all this to happen.

I think this inability to describe what deep depression is really like is not just my own. Some of the great poets like Dante and Milton and Donne and George Herbert, as well as Oscar Wilde in *The Ballad of Reading Gaol*, do capture, or at least echo, some of it. Even the great depths of Psalm 130, the *de profundis* psalm, do not really mean much to me; although the Latin words *de profundis* ('out of the depths') do, simply because they are low in sound and reverberate rather like the notes on a cello, one of the few kinds of music that can reach me. In the same way the only artists who seem to understand the experience of depression are some of the old masters, particularly Rembrandt with his dark shadows.

2

It has been well said by the late Neville Ward that when we are in pain we must try to avoid the contraction of our world to that point where pain is all that there seems to be.[1] The trouble is that you can deal with ordinary physical pain and sickness in your mind and in prayer to some extent. But when you are depressed, that part of you which should be able to deal with adversity is just not functioning, so that Neville Ward's words do not mean anything logical. There is nothing that is logical. There is no such thing as logic and, what is much worse, there is no such thing as love. There is really just nothing at all except this hideous and dreadful nothingness. In some ways it is like being down in a deep, dark well. It is not only a well of loneliness, but a well in which there is no light and no hope of escape at all. You are just down there with an awful sense of dread. It is not a dread of anything in particular that can be identified. As I said before, it is literally dread-full. There is also a sense of being profoundly confused and of not understanding what is going on at all. I don't think it has much to do with faith, or even the lack of it, because as far as I can see, my faith, in orthodox terms, was not affected during this time. I was able to say my Office and to do some intercession; but there was a dreadful sense of confusion and the total inability to think clearly, or even to think at all.

The Voice of the Psalms

The one verse in the Psalms that spoke to me at my lowest point was Psalm 107:

> Such as sit in darkness and in the shadow of death: being fast bound in misery and iron.[2]

That just about sums it up—you are bound fast in misery and iron and there is no way out or hope of escape at all. Of course there were other verses of the Psalms which echoed

---

[1] cf. *The Use of Praying*, Ch. 8, 'Suffering', Epworth Press, 1967.
[2] The Book of Common Prayer translation of the Psalms is used throughout.

my situation in various ways, but I cannot really recall them at all; nor do I quite understand why they were of particular help to me. For instance, there was Psalm 19: 3:

> There is neither speech nor language: but their voices are heard among them.

For me those voices were the voices of creation itself, which speaks of the glory of God, though it has neither speech nor language; and also the voices of the psalmists and the saints, and, of course, Job. In all these was the voice of God.

Then there is Psalm 130 to which I have already referred. It begins 'Out of the deep', *De profundis*:

> Out of the deep have I called unto thee, O Lord.

At the time I preferred to say 'Out of the depths ...' Then, as far as I can remember, as I gradually began to emerge from the depths, verses 2 and 3 of Psalm 69 meant a lot to me:

> I stick fast in the deep mire, where no ground is: I am come into deep waters, so that the floods run over me.
>
> I am weary of crying; my throat is dry: my sight faileth me for waiting so long upon my God.

My eyes were affected, and I still find reading and watching television a little difficult. Also in the same psalm, verses 13 to 19 were important to me:

> But, Lord, I make my prayer unto thee: in an acceptable time.
>
> Hear me, O God, in the multitude of thy mercy: even in the truth of thy salvation.
>
> Take me out of the mire, that I sink not: O let me be delivered from them that hate me, and out of the deep waters.
>
> Let not the water-flood drown me, neither let the deep swallow me up: and let not the pit shut her mouth upon me.

> Hear me, O Lord, for thy loving-kindness is comfortable: turn thee unto me according to the multitude of thy mercies.
>
> And hide not thy face from thy servant, for I am in trouble: O haste thee, and hear me.
>
> Draw nigh unto my soul, and save it: O deliver me, because of my enemies.

That phrase, 'multitude of mercy', makes a lovely deep sound and is repeated elsewhere in the Psalms, e.g. Ps. 5: 7 and Ps. 51: 1. As I gradually began the long haul back, Ps. 27: 16 came into focus: 'O tarry thou the Lord's leisure ...' It all seemed to be taking so very long. Then, as I began very slowly to emerge out of utter blackness, other verses of this same psalm began to take on some reality for me, particularly as I started looking forward to the possibility of celebrating the Eucharist again, which I had not been able to do for several months. I had been able to receive Holy Communion both in hospital and at home, and that was good. The Eucharist itself, the offering and pleading of the great sacrifice of Christ, upon the Cross and then risen and glorified, is a great deal more than machinery for producing Holy Communion, even though I have never really known this through actual experience. As I began to think about the real possibility of presiding at the Eucharist once more, Psalm 27: 7-10 started to light up again.

> Therefore will I offer in his dwelling an oblation with great gladness: I will sing, and speak praises unto the Lord.
>
> Hearken unto my voice, O Lord, when I cry unto thee: have mercy upon me, and hear me.
>
> My heart hath talked of thee, Seek ye my face: Thy face, Lord, will I seek.
>
> O hide not thou thy face from me: nor cast thy servant away in displeasure.

As I started getting better I found more and more that individual psalm verses I had previously not registered as having any special meaning began to light up for me. I really began to see I was feeling alive again when I found I could make sense of these two verses at the end of Psalm 30:

> Thou hast turned my heaviness into joy: thou hast put off my sackcloth, and girded me with gladness.
>
> Therefore shall every good man sing of thy praise without ceasing: O my God, I will give thanks unto thee for ever.

There came a day when I wanted to reclaim Psalm 37: 32:

> The law of his God is in his heart: and his goings shall not slide.

The law of God had at one time been in my heart, but latterly it had just been in my memory, and I very much wanted not just to be obedient, but to have that true obedience springing from my heart again.

One of the Psalms that I say every day because it is set as an introductory psalm for Morning Prayer is Psalm 95, commonly known as the *Venite*. It begins:

> O come let us sing unto the Lord: let us heartily rejoice in the strength of our salvation.

Obviously 'singing' and 'rejoicing' did not mean anything much, but the word 'strength' did. It comes again in verse 4:

> In his hand are all the corners of the earth [including this tight corner I am now shut up in]: and the strength of the hills is his also.

It was that strength that I could dimly set against my own weakness and, if only I could make it real, upon which I could depend.

The Glory of God

In the Book of Common Prayer a rubric states that at the end of every psalm the short *Gloria* should be repeated:

Glory be to the Father, and to the Son: and to the Holy Ghost [although nowadays I prefer to say 'and to the Holy Spirit of God']; As it was in the beginning, is now and ever shall be: world without end. Amen.

I found that this was quite unexpectedly helpful. One can wonder about, and wonder at, the glory of God 'as it was in the beginning', before there was any creation. Just God in all his glory. Yet God was not a single Being in all that glory. As the opening of St John's Gospel proclaims: 'In the beginning was the Word, and the Word was with God, and the Word was God.' There was also the Holy Spirit. So there is God in all his Triune Majesty and in all his Love and transcendent Beauty.

Then the *Gloria* states that that same glory is not just 'in the beginning', but also 'is now'. That is the bit to hang onto in depression. The glory is still there, although you just cannot see it or feel it, or even begin to know it. But the Church knows it, and it is very worthwhile repeating that assertion with the Church, even though at the time you do not wholly believe in it. The final statement is that that same glory 'ever shall be, world without end.' I sometimes wonder about that. I myself am inclined to believe that God's glory in the end may even (*per impossibile*) have been increased by the fact of the glorious redemption of humanity and the whole creation by the birth, death and resurrection of the Son of God, our Lord and Saviour Jesus Christ. However impossible this may sound, the Athanasian Creed does speak of Christ 'taking the manhood into God', so that it seems that it is not impossible for God to add to his glory.

The Descent into Hell

There is also one sentence in the Apostles' Creed which sounded really loud and true and clear to me, repeated as it is at Morning and Evening Prayer in the Church of England: 'He descended into hell'—and hell was indeed where I was or felt myself to be, right down in the depths amongst the dead.

I was not in Gehenna, the place of burning, but in Hades, the place of the departed, of the shades, of darkness, and of the living dead. I often wonder why it is that this particular statement, 'He descended into hell', does not come into the Nicene Creed which we use at the Eucharist. This seems to me to be a considerable loss. In places where the Apostles' Creed is not normally used, congregations will become less and less familiar with the fact that our Lord did descend into hell (cf. 1 Pet 3: 18-20). He descends into the hell in which the depressed person is, too. Not that we can feel or know his presence there with us, but we do know that he has experienced it; he knows what it is like to be in hell.

The two set collects for Morning Prayer in the Book of Common Prayer are very valuable, clearly envisaging us as being surrounded by enemies:

> Defend us thy humble servants from all assaults of our enemies that we, surely trusting in Thy defence may not fear the power of any adversaries.

and:

> Defend us in the same with Thy mighty power.

The set collects for Evening Prayer also envisage us in the same miserable condition of being beset by evil powers around us:

> Lighten our darkness, we beseech thee, O Lord; and by thy great mercy defend us from all perils and dangers of this night; for the love of thy only Son, our Saviour, Jesus Christ.

The night of depression is fraught with dangers and darkness and all manner of adversaries and perils.

There is a comforting thought which has to do not only with the Psalms, although it is very prominent there, but with the whole of the Old Testament as the history of Israel. The Old Testament is the story of how the people of God, chosen and led and favoured by him, constantly rebelled against him in arrogant and flagrant ways. Yet again and again they returned to him, by reason of the 'multitude of his mercies'. God has entered into covenant with them—in modern terms we would call this a 'peace-pact' or a 'defence alliance'—and however much that covenant is broken by God's people, God will never break it. The Old Covenant has been renewed through the New Covenant in Christ. It is a Covenant with us and with the whole of creation, the Church and all Christian people at its heart. Belief in the unbreakable Covenant of God with his people can stand one in good stead in times of utmost despair.

Biblical Material

I think there is probably a very great deal of Biblical material available to those who are in difficulty or depression. I haven't the ability to deal with it and draw it all together, but I am sure that a scheme of daily regular Bible reading is of great value, and quite unexpected things pop up in both the Old and New Testaments.

The book of Job meant a lot to me at this time. I don't get much help from his so-called comforters, but the direct conversations between God and Job towards the end of the book are quite magnificent. I have always had a fellow-feeling for Job, because he not only experienced very considerable diminishment in every way, but clearly suffered from a good many rather nasty diseases, one of which must have been something akin to the psoriasis that has afflicted me for most of my life.

One of the little things that pops up for me from the Old Testament is a memorable sentence from the prophet Habakkuk: 'I will joy in the God of my salvation' (3: 18); or, as one modern paraphrase has it, 'I will joy in God my Jesus'. There are lots of lovely bits, and it is worthwhile reading slowly through a lot of rather dull stuff. You will stumble across hidden things that perhaps mean something to you personally but which other folk may not recognize as anything out of the ordinary. I am deeply grateful that I was able to say the Office almost every day throughout my depression, not least because it enabled me to gather up these invaluable fragments from the Scriptures. I wish I could claim that it was my religion that made this possible, but it was mainly because I am, amongst other things, obsessionally neurotic, and just cannot let some things go—in this case a very good thing!

I am not sure how much of this will be of use to anyone who has not been accustomed to daily prayer and Bible reading. All I can recommend to someone who is not used to doing this is to try to remember any little bits you do know—even if it is only the Lord's Prayer or Psalm 23; or a prayer that you learned as a child or have picked up since then—and go on saying them. There is great value in repeating something, almost anything, that has to do with God and which has a good sound or cadence or rhythm about it. Such things are easily distinguishable from the 'vain repetitions' against which our Lord warned us, and the great advantage of familiarity with them is that they can reach down to us even in the deadness of depression.

My Personal Diagnosis

It is time to return to trying to understand and deal with the massive depression itself. I have mentioned two immediate factual causes of my recent depression, my retirement from active work and my time in hospital for rather traumatic surgery. So this was to some extent a 'reactive depression', that is to say, a subconscious reaction against these things. I am inclined to agree with the psychiatrist Dr Frank Lake, who claims that reactive depression stems from repressed rage or anger. I did not realize it then, but I imagine that I must have been subconsciously very angry—presumably with God—at having to give up my work and my status, with all its privileges, and retire into comparative obscurity. I was angry too at the fact that I had to go through a good deal of pain, and at all the indignities of being in hospital, being washed and cleaned and fed and sometimes treated like a recalcitrant child—which, in effect, I had become. All this was quite enough to cause a pretty strong and deep depression. Perhaps I should have been more alert to, and aware of, all these factors, but I wasn't.

Deeper down, and underlying the reactive depression, was the fact that I was diagnosed a good number of years ago as an endogenous depressive. I do not understand the full clinical meaning of this, but the word 'endogenous' means 'from within': that is to say, it has its origins from within oneself, as contrasted with a reactive depression which has its origins in something from outside oneself. Reactive depression happens when one is facing something over which one has no control, such as needing to retire or having to undergo surgery or suffering bereavement.

This diagnosis of endogenous depression was made by a very competent psychiatrist after a long consultation. He took into account not only my condition at the time, but also the fact that I had had a number of catatonic seizures throughout my life. These were not spectacular; they were simply occasions on which I quite unconsciously contracted out and became generally unable to do anything, except just lie there in a not unpleasant kind of coma. These episodes lasted sometimes for several hours and sometimes for days. The psychiatrist explained this by saying that there was something in my brain that was not functioning properly. He likened it to what happens when somebody has diabetes and the pancreas is not functioning properly. The patient has to be given insulin in order to keep alive, but with the right treatment, he or she can indeed live a perfectly healthy and good life. So the psychiatrist explained that my brain needed an anti-depressant, not a tranquilizer, to supply what was lacking.

Throughout the years, I have been on various anti-depressants, because new ones become available as research goes on, and they have enabled me under normal circumstances to perform adequately. But, of course, when a reactive depression comes on top of an endogenous one, then the person tends to go to pieces, as I did. Moreover, the doctors had to withdraw my anti-depressant tablets while I was in hospital, because they had a side-effect of reducing my immunity to infection. I say all this because some of you reading this who are suffering from depression *may*, and I stress *may*, have an endogenous tendency underlying it all, and it is worth finding out. I was on a television programme about depression a number of years ago in which a doctor admitted the fact that, although he had been in general practice for some twenty years, he really knew nothing about the cause or treatment of depression. I do not know if this is generally the case, but it may be worthwhile pressing for a consultation with a psychiatrist.

My most recent psychiatrist has a slightly different picture of what it is all about, compared with the psychiatrist of thirty to forty years ago. She says that the synapses in my brain are not functioning properly and I need something to enable them to do so. But whichever picture of endogenous depression is right, it is a very great comfort to know that it has a diagnosable physical basis or cause, and that it is not just my own fault that I am so very depressed. It is likewise reassuring to know that it is no more reprehensible to be 'on' anti-depressants than it is to be 'on' insulin if you are a diabetic.

Bereavement

It has been suggested to me, and I think rightly, that retirement has some features akin to bereavement, in that both involve the loss of something, or someone, rightly valued and treasured. In my own case I had never really let myself consciously experience bereavement or dealt with it adequately, if at all. This was one of the reasons why I dealt so inadequately with retirement. To put it very broadly, my mother left us children when we were very young (a 'bereavement' which I did not recognize as such), and when she died later on, I did not even attend her funeral. This took place in another country, but I could have been there for it if I had really made the effort. I wish now that I had done so. My father died in England while I was in South Africa, and I was not told of his death until months afterwards. My sister, whom I had badly neglected to help through an unhappy marriage, died suddenly in hospital. Again I didn't know until after the event, though I did manage to get to her funeral. My younger brother died on the island of Pemba, near Zanzibar, and again I only heard of that some months afterwards. So, partly through my own fault and partly through circumstances, I never grieved for my family, most of whom I hardly knew. I am sure that this lack of grieving and of a sense of bereavement had a connection with my inadequacy when I had a real sense of 'bereavement' at the loss of my work.

Sleeplessness

Another feature of this last depression, a feature rather than a factor, was that I had a long bout of sleeplessness. A disturbed sleep pattern is a very common symptom of depression and I had had just such a pattern for years, generally waking up very early in the morning and sleeping very fitfully. But this was something very different. I was on sleeping tablets at the time, but they were designed only to give me a couple of hours' sleep, the idea being that I would then continue to sleep under my own steam, as it were. I used to go to bed at 10 p.m. and then wake up at about midnight or 1 a.m. and just not be able to get back to sleep. At first I used to toss and turn in my bed until I was aware this would not help. So I used to get up in my pyjamas and go into the living room and sit on the sofa or wander about.

During these long hours I kept having what I can only describe as hallucinations. They were not nightmares. I am very familiar with nightmares, having had them ever since I was a child, and in recent years I have even woken up other people in the same house by screaming or shouting. What I was experiencing now was something very different. I can't describe these hallucinations very clearly because I do not remember what they were, except that I seemed to be constantly being jostled about by a great crowd of people in some enclosed space like a supermarket or an underground station. A friend of mine, who lives on the floor beneath me (and to whom I owe more than I can ever say for her consistent care of me), sometimes heard me crashing around in the dark and would come up and talk with me during these bouts; this would comfort me and quieten me down. I shall never forget the first good night's sleep I had after all this. It was the night following the day on which my current psychiatrist came to visit me. What she did or said in that brief half-hour visit I have no idea. But afterwards I slept like a log—thanks be to God!

Perhaps I should digress at this point to consider briefly a question that is sometimes of concern to religious people when they are looking for help from a psychiatrist. As far as I know my psychiatrist is not herself a Christian. The question of religion obviously cropped up quite a lot, but she never revealed her own religious standpoint. The reason I mention this is because some people say that they would prefer to go to a Christian psychiatrist; though I can understand this, I do not personally think it really matters. What one needs and wants is a competent psychiatrist, whatever his or her religious persuasion may be. The days are gone when psychiatrists tended to look down their noses at religion and even to regard religious belief as some kind of aberration. If it has any reality or validity, one's religion is an integral part of one's own life experience, and it would be a very inexperienced therapist or psychiatrist who disregarded it. So do not worry if a psychiatrist to whom you might be sent is not a practising Christian—all that you need to know is that he or she is competent.

After that unforgettable first good night's sleep, and with subsequent regular weekly visits from the psychiatrist, I began to get better. This period of the beginning of recovery was characterized by an appalling feeling of total apathy and a complete lack of interest. I didn't want to see anybody or to do anything. I could not summon up enough energy or interest even to watch television, far less to read. When I did eventually begin to read again, all I could manage were thrillers. The idea of reading anything better was utterly out of the question. I think the first books of any real substance that I tackled, and then read avidly, were Philip Toynbee's two autobiographical journals, *Part of a Journey* (Collins, 1981) and *End of a Journey* (Hamish Hamilton, 1989). Philip Toynbee was himself a depressive, and it is always a help to read something by somebody who has been through it all. It is for this reason that I have struggled in these few pages to describe something of my own experience of depression, even though much of it remains so meaningless and confused, in the hope that it may speak to someone who is similarly afflicted, or to a friend who is trying to help someone else out of the depths.

As I said earlier, one of the things that I found helpful when I was myself in the depths was the voice of the Psalms. That was a voice I could hear, and I hope that others suffering from depression will find that the Psalms, or something similar, will speak to them. Perhaps I may conclude with one last short psalm that I found came to have tremendous significance for me, Psalm 61. Here are the first four verses:

> Hear my crying, O God: give ear unto my prayer.
>
> From the ends of the earth will I call upon thee: when my heart is in heaviness.
>
> O set me up upon the rock that is higher than I: for thou hast been my hope, and a strong tower for me against the enemy.
>
> I will dwell in thy tabernacle for ever: and my trust shall be under the covering of thy wings.

Although I was totally unable to recognize it when I first used this psalm in my depression, I have since begun to see that the deep shadow of darkness which I was experiencing was not only the darkness of the absence of God, but also the darkness of the presence of God who, even in the depths, is faithful. 'Under the covering of thy wings' has come to mean something of this to me. I believe that all who suffer even the deepest darkness are under the covering of God's wings.

EPILOGUE

'Melancholy is too painful, it reaches too deeply into the roots of human existence to permit us to leave it to the psychiatrists ... we believe there is a question here of something closely related to the depths of human nature,' says Romano Guardini in his paper on 'The Meaning of Melancholy' (in *The Focus of Freedom*, Dublin, Helicon, 1966, p. 55). How right he is, and how good it is to have Canon Gonville ffrench-Beytagh writing for us here, as a Christian priest, from the depths of his own experience of human nature and the painful bouts of depression he suffers, yet able to express his gratitude to the psychiatrists too.

Many of you who read this will not have the profound pleasure of knowing Gonville personally, so I want to say a little about him to provide a context for the depths of what he tells us here. Depression is not the first word that would spring to mind about him—that's why his ruthless honesty is so moving. He is a rounded and rumbustious person—robust in faith, racy in speech, trenchant in views. He is excellent company on any conceivable occasion, from the depths of shared, silent, contemplative prayer or the profundity of his absorption in the celebration of the Eucharist, to the laughter, relaxation and ease of good conversations over the whisky, to being able to speak from the heart and have a good cry into his supply of tissues.

Friends will know that whenever I am asked to say what a priest should be like, I start describing Gonville. He holds great opposites in creative play in his person. Equally at home in the catholicity of the Church and the complexity of the world, he's both street-wise (he loves cities) and wise in the things of God. He can cut through cant to the quick of the human heart with an unerring accuracy and depth of compassion. He is one of the great preachers. His sermons and talks are a delight—full of wisdom and intriguing ideas, always interesting (Gonville is incapable of being boring) and capable of changing you profoundly. You never know with Gonville when God will suddenly have you by the throat or by the heart.

He is also, in spite of all his disavowals, a very brave man. His stance as an involved Christian witness in relation to social and political evils took him to prison in South Africa. To understand more about this and the story of his earlier life do read his book *Encountering Darkness*.[3] When we reflect on what he has done, alongside what he has felt and suffered, as touched on in this present pamphlet, it makes us aware again that sanity and sanctity are not the same thing, thank God.

Above all Gonville believes centrally in the love of God— and knows that it is only love that can make any sense at all in the inalienable pains and anguish of this world. He knows that it is a love that has to be lived out practically in the teeth of all the evidence to the contrary. He is a passionate man and when you are with him you soon learn what matters to him— God and you, and what you are doing about God. Many lives have been much changed by Gonville's ministry, and mine amongst them. He not only made me take God more seriously, more intimately, he also made me take the visible Church and our sacramental needs more seriously too. Since meeting Gonville, I find that even in my worst moments I can only bring myself to say that I am permanently on the way out of the Church. At best he has helped me to belong, and to find infinite, eternal riches in commitment. I love and admire the way in which his firm espousal of the truths of the faith and the strengths of the tradition makes him *free*, deep and generous, affirming yet demanding, in his humanity and his being with others, no matter where they are.

Some of you who read this will recognize your own experience as being like Gonville's and will feel met by him in

_____

[3] *Encountering Darkness*, Collins, 1973.

the lonely places. Like him you may have had to find the necessary humility at times to know that you need medication to help you to survive and hull the depression out. The way in which he talks about prayer and reading that can keep you in existence, that can just simply 'hold' the situation a little, is profoundly and practically helpful.

Others who read this will know that your experiences of depression are not always quite the same as his. There is a continuum of depressed moods that stretches from ordinary, everyday feelings of sadness to dreadful states of feeling damned and cast out for ever from God's mercy. We have to acknowledge that different things can help at various stages in this continuum. Pastoral counsellors, psychotherapists, psychologists, as well as those involved in pastoral ministries and spiritual companionship of various kinds, will all know that many of us can be helped out of depressive attitudes and thought patterns about life, or can be helped in the management of depressed moods. In our depressions we all need some assistance in discerning what is really going on, in order to know what help it is appropriate to seek.

In the human experience of depression there is a great challenge to the Church generally, and to theologians in particular, to take the meaning of feelings, moods, more seriously. The tradition shies away from their inconstancy. Yet moods recur. They are constant in their inconstancy and are indicators of where we are, how we are, who we are, in relation to our own embodied being, to our being in the body of our social world and in the Body of Christ. Moods are about states of being that are common to all human experience and have, therefore, deep meaning and significance in our relation to God and to each other.

Depressed moods plunge us into feelings of the loss of significance, of value, of meaning, that are like a state of bereavement, an awareness of absence rather than presence of what was once present and loved. As the mood deepens, feeling-sensations (often with a bodily component) of emptiness, darkness, tiredness, inertia, capitulation grow into a state of bleak, dreary helplessness and hopelessness. As someone once said to me, 'It is not a matter of no light at the end of the tunnel, it's that I can't even believe there is a tunnel. I am lost.' Part of the experience is also that of self-hating, self-tormenting guilt. The sufferer feels bad and in the wrong. We must take great care to realize that this guilt becomes increasingly not contrition about the things done and undone that are wrong and need amendment, but a guilt that is an existential guilt about the fact that one exists at all—it is guilt about being. That is why in depressed moods we tend to want to apologize for our existence, as we feel such an intolerable burden to others. It also helps us to understand why part of the suicidal thinking in depression takes the form of feeling that others will really be better off without us.

A certain degree of depression *is* the human response to *loss*—whether, for example, of a loved person, of the usual sense of selfhood, of habitual ways of doing something. So, for instance, bereavement, losses of jobs, changes in church forms and rituals, are all examples of the kind of loss that make us feel depressed, till we have readjusted. The way in which we organize our corporate life does not always leave enough room for working through the natural history of these processes.

Some people have very early experiences of separation, loss, abandonment, exclusion, abusive assaults on the person—either physical or 'moral'—when they are too young to be conscious of what is happening. The experiences are too traumatic to be integrated and leave fearful patterns of expectation that are easily touched off again in later intimate relationships. They also leave deep wounds and defensive scar tissue that have built up as a way of surviving. The inner world for people with this kind of early background contains a recurring potential for experiences of inner loss of a good sense of the self and the 'other', so that depression is all too common an experience. (Gonville's brief account of his childhood in this pamphlet illustrates something of what I mean.) In a deep therapeutic, healing, and trustworthy relationship with another human being, some of these traumatic experiences can sometimes be worked with in such a way as to integrate them into a more mature and less defensive experience of self. It is usually long and painful work—how could it be otherwise, when such depths of human anguish are involved? All true healing comes from God, but he needs us to incarnate his love so that people can feel it and believe it and learn to use it.

We need to develop a more adequate theology of what a viable self-love and self-respect are about. The struggle with depression is sometimes intensified for Christians, who are taught so much about self-loss or dying to self that they cannot hold their corner in the interaction between love of God, love of neighbour, love of self, all of which are intimately bound up together. You cannot give away, or sacrifice, what you never had in the first place. You cannot surrender your self if you cannot experience the fact that you have one or are one. Many Christians are hooked into forms of workaholism, the fallacy of proving your value by what you do or achieve; or forms of endless appeasing, placatory relationships; or patterns of compulsive care-giving, which are all based on a depressed sense of the self. How can we learn in our life together to mediate the unconditional love of God for us, that looks on our createdness and sees it as 'altogether good and beautiful' (Gen. 1: 31) and helps us to deal with what is amiss by reconciling us to God and each other in the gift of his Son?

In our experiences of depression we have to learn to be liberation theologians. We have to learn to stop identifying with the victim-self in our experience. We have to help the victim to stand up and work with God and others for better ways in relationships. We have to help the victim-self to have the courage to question and get into dialogue with the internal critic, the put-down oppressor, who casts an idolatrous shadow over how we experience God, whose love is without limits.

For many there is much that can be done—by the self in loving, exploratory relationships with others and with God—in these all-too-human experiences of depression. But sometimes it goes too deep. Gonville knows that. Then we have to alleviate what we can by medication or other means in order to survive and throw ourselves into the mercy of God.

The Psalms, the story of Job, the experiences of many of the prophets, the Garden of Gethsemane and the Passion of Christ, and the life stories of the saints and mystics who have learnt what it means to become 'partakers of the divine nature', all remind us how deeply the experiences of 'loss' resonate in the experience of being human in relation to the mystery of the reality of God. Experiences of darkness, depression, dereliction are so much a part of maturing into the depths of friendship with God. We need people who can be true to their experience and share it with us. Thus in our human experiences of depression, in spite of all the temptations to give up on life, we may be enabled through God's mercy to hold onto existence and cling to God, who is there and who is Love, whether we know it through his presence, or his felt 'absence'. In the end this Love makes us take on, in all its awesome depths, the gift of human freedom.

Thank you, Gonville, for your shared companionship on the way.

WENDY ROBINSON
Oxford 1990